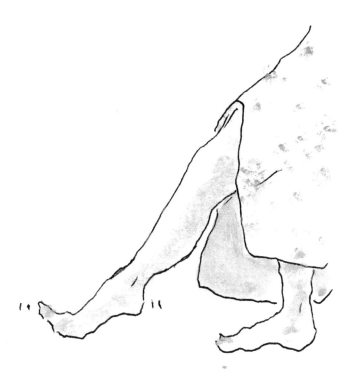

the old lady peasant
in hospital

I came to this country from Holland in 1979 with my late husband and two sons, After a career in interior design and fashion, we started a small farm in Devon. I studied oil painting in Holland but switched to sculpture after my husband's death in 2001. My sculptures have featured regularly in local galleries and 'open studios'.

In 2017, I suddenly felt an urge to put my thoughts and every-day adventures into light hearted rhyme with simple illustrations. With the help and support of Jack, the dog, and the indespensable Rob (boots size 10), every Saturday and loads of optimism, I keep on enjoying it all.

Copyright © 2018 Michele Meyer
www.michelemeyer.net

Text and Illustrations by Michele Meyer
Cover Design by Michele Meyer
Formatted by Ventura Creative Projects

Printed by CreateSpace

ISBN: 9781792092855

CONTENTS

by page

A pimple on my leg

Got a pimple on my leg
And, for a while, thought what the heck!
After months of such neglect
To the doctor for a check.

He is precise
And no surprise
Eagerly writes something down
Saying with a hint of frown:

'I give you a month, ok'

Not too alarming, isn't it
Unless, it's the doc who is saying it
My eyes widen, open mouth
As I hear the doctor shout:

'It's the prescription for your pill
No need to think about your will!'

Conclusions made in split of second,
Too alarming, I would reckon.
Just a minute on the clock
Could prevent a nasty shock

Goodbye to skiing

We did go skiing all my life
To the family's delight!
In Luxembourg I met the kids
And saw the Dermatologist.
He sorted dent and tiny pimple,
Froze them off, that was quite simple.

The end of skiing did appear
With more caution.... and some fear,
And at seventy I said:
'Sorry, I am too old for that'!
No more trip to darling kids
And no more Dermatologist.

Moving on, two years have passed.
Things are changing pretty fast!
I started rhyming, writing verses,
And see Doctor, cancer nurses.
I met new people with their stories
All excitement and no worries!
Life, I live intensively,
So much beauty there to see!

You can read on and do not worry
I am here to tell the story.........

Needles and wasps

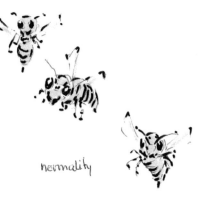

normality

Autumn is coming to the farm
There just is a slight alarm
Is my 'pimple', not so good?
Another doctor, another look
Another scan, another cut
That should be it...but...

First the needles now it's wasps!
Our paths have rarely crossed
They want a nice and gentle place
To do things at a slower pace.
End of season, autumn 's come
For the wasps, their work is done.
On my hand, meandering
They have lost the will to sting.

short
peaceful
phase

Observing thus, they make me ask:
Is it really our task
To go on and on and wait
Until that late
To lose our sting and strive
For a serene and peaceful life?

death

More about the pimple

More doctors, more injections
And, on reflection,
The battle is not done
It's only just begun.

I joked about my 'Pimple'
Thought it would be simple
Just cosmetic, cut and out
Nothing more to think about.

My 'Pimple' makes me lead
A different life indeed.
The sheep I see sporadically
The cows would like a chat with me.

The geese, I talk to so much more
As they wait at kitchen door.

Thus, we do discuss....

Life's joy and happiness
And decide it would be best
To gather around my kitchen table
With lots of friends we would be able
To rejoice in fun and laughter
Having lots of tea thereafter.
That could be it, all it takes,
Just baking loads of lovely cakes.

Choices ...or getting older

A peasant as no other
Has an undemanding cover.
Acting like a kind of curtain
When hesitating and uncertain.
Which way is right, where shall I go?
So many choices can't do all!

There is the sculpting and the farming
Kept the bees with sting... alarming!
I tend to chickens, cows and sheep
And my special friends the geese
And then there is the poeting,
Yet another silly thing.

Choice and uncertainty
Are chasing me increasingly.
Advancing years should make it easy?
But, no, it isn't easy peasy!
Will I have the strength to go
To hold and help and ailing cow?
Which doctor will I visit next?
Treatments getting more complex!

After tea and contemplation
It's simplicity... determination,
Baking bread to share with friends
Is where my ambition ends!
Fitting in most perfectly
With my peasant imagery.

Controlling cells

I had a longish e-mail talk
With my nephew in New York.
He researches cells
Is clever,... he excels!
He hasn't given up on me...
... (can happen in a family)!

He hatches out a clever plot
To help and stop
A really very nasty cell
That wants to dwell
And take control,
Not such good news at all.

They can't take that control from me
I like to be in charge, you see.
You might think it rather sneaky
And controlling somewhat freaky.
But there we have it, to be fair
That seems to be my character!

Hospital or hospital

Big Hospital and wait in queue
... or jump it ... what to do?
There is a smaller one next door
With nice nick-nacks and confort. ← (French spelling)

Not insured, I pay a fee
When I go there privately.
Registered as 'Charity'
They tend to charge abundantly.

You might be getting extra care
Not paying any parking fare,
Free coffee in a porcelain cup
And well dressed nurses turning up!

Will it be my destiny
Sneaking off continuously
For a charge free parking place
And see my doctor face to face?

Initiative or free parking

I never was extremely fast,
But when it matters....... blast!

Did free parking do the trick?
... met my surgeon and it clicked!
No need to pussyfoot about,
We better get the scalpel out.

And on his own initiative
.....just in a whiff
He fixed a date...
And I surely wouldn't be late!

In the theatre

Once in the operating room
They put you under pretty soon.
In Theatre and on the table
I'm out of it and quite unable
To witness with a conscious mind
A performance so refined!

There is to come a great reward
Being taken to my ward.
All the action down in there
Is the best of theatre!
Love, pain and loads of action,
Courage, service and affection...
And one thing theatre can't be
Just the plain reality.

The operation

My operation went so well,
My skillful surgeon came to tell.
Got it out my nasty pest
In a lump, with all the rest.
Oh, I am a happy bunny
... be it with a lighter tummy;
And the leg is done as well
Just a clean and empty dell!

Waiting time was rather long
Worth it though ... don't get me wrong!
The right time for a puzzle game
My Sudoku tests the brain,
But as I try it seems in vain
... the printers got it wrong again!

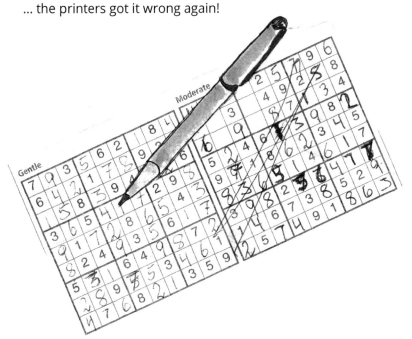

On my ward

On my ward I lay with pleasure
Looking round, observe at leisure,
The colourful variety
In ailments, strength, ability.

H4, my designated bed,
In H5 by chance I met
Margaret, whom I like a lot.
Her remarks just hit the spot!

Occasionally I ran past her
A poem I made earlier.
And listen she did patiently
No choice there, no mobility!

Her mind was keen, her brain so sharp,
We thought that life was just a lark!
With ups and downs, admitted,
Laughs generally permitted!

We kept in touch, she is like me,
A case the doctors like to see.
And again we have the pleasure
To watch proceedings at our leisure.

Visits

My friends, they come to visit me
And instantly I see
The faintest smile around the mouth
But in their eyes there is no doubt
... tragic fear...
...the end is near!
Is that a setting by default
Or being earnest.... And no joke.

They seem to need some cheering up
And I might help, they are in luck!
I can do the 'happy blighter'
Until the atmosphere gets lighter.

By the time they leave again
I am exhausted... grab the pen
To record the fun and laughter
May it stay for ever after
And the love they gave to me
In endless generosity.

The fire alarm

Moving round in all directions
Without perceivable direction....
On my ward in bed H2
A patient has those symptoms too.
She struggles making sense of it
I struggle just observing it.

That was an illness and no kidding
But at times it is transmitting
Into life's 'normality'.
To me it happens frequently
When I use the mobile phone
Or try to get the chickens home,
Or reading out the clear instructions
For Ikea's bright constructions.
Or try to stop the smoke alarm
Swinging round a desperate arm!

Moving round in all directions
Without perceivable direction...
From our rulers it's accepted
Once established and elected.
With mobile phones they are at ease
But look for shelter if you please
.... When fire starts don't trust their arm
To safely reach the smoke alarm!

Red Leicester

Luncheon finishes with cheese
Life is full of luxuries!
I look at it, I've got the time,
A prefect square, all in line.
Packaging got so efficient
My trying finger seems to miss it!
Opening a hellish pain
... I try and try....and try again.
It's Red Leicester
.... if you get there!

And then, ...surprisingly,
In tiny print, I just can see.
It's imported from NL!
Do I feel responsible
For the colour, taste or texture?
It's deceivingly like Leicester.

But when it comes to opening
Surely there the Dutch come in.
They exploit its main attraction:
.... anticipation, without question!

The pirate patch

I bought myself a pirate patch
And a second one to match.
They are joined up in the middle
To avoid an awkward fiddle.
I will put them on at night
Not to see the ceiling light.

Enlightenment... so overrated
When switching off is so belated!
Pirates wear just only one
Leaves the choice.... bright or dumb.

Brian the storm

The storms, they blow increasingly
With more and more intensity.
You have them named for A to Z
Now it's Brian we are at.
He does effect the birds in flight
Tearing up the errant kite,
Melting bits of polar ice
And making our rivers rise,
Dealing out horrendous blows
To all the systems as he goes.

I blame Brian for the fact
That my pen is going mad.
Creative fluids are in flood,
You better put the flood gates up
I wouldn't like to let you drown
In floods of words I am writing down!

My Pico... R.i.P.

My Pico is a thing quite smashing
Small, white with green lights flashing,
Attached to me so bodily
Pressurising constantly
To drain the operation site.
I guess he does that with delight
Competing with the drainage pipe
For prime position on the site.

I had for ever to untie
My entangled upper thigh.
Oh ...there is no denying it
We really were quite intimate!
He should be out, dead by day five
... he wasn't.... still very much alive!

Now they say they take him out
And just dump him, without doubt!
On hearing all about his fate
He decided, not to late
"There is no use in being smashing"
And stopped his little green lights flashing.

Pico No.2

Still mourning Pico's sad demise
I was really quite surprised
When Pico number two was fitted
Nurses tried and tried ... then did it.

But Pico two was not too happy
With angry bleeping he just said it.
Overworked and leaking air.
A third nurse tried a brave repair.
Then Doctor come, said: "oh"
"This seems to be the status quo"!

Seen the leak in our attachment
With Pico two I feel detachment.
Angry bleeping, wire muddle,
It was a loud and angry struggle!
All of this made little sense
.... Until a nurse with confidence
Tells him with authority
To stop his games immediately.

Digestive biscuits

It was precisely 3 o'clock
When I heard a little knock.
A seagull on the windowsill
Had to feed her, come what will
Three Digestives' what she ate
Said thanks and that was that!

An episode I would forget
Was it not, however, that
It was again at three o' clock
The next day, another knock!
Same procedure once again
Makes me wonder that a brain
Fitting in a tiny head
Can remember not forget,
The time and quality of feed!
What a miracle indeed!

Shrink with age is what I do
And my brain will do that too,
But the gull gives me some hope
.... A tiny brain has still some scope!

Goodbye

Tomorrow will be my release
Going home, a great relief!
I hope they rid me of my cancer
But only later comes the answer.

To say goodbye is always sad,
But they will use my empty bed
To change this lovely entity
Enriching its variety.
My time with you, as I recall
Was never ever sad at all!
And all I can and need to do
Is sincerely thanking you.

Brownie points or being a patient

To get about and live and thrive
That's the easy part of life.
But when you start with ills and sickness
You need full strength and fighting fitness
Life wouldn't be the same again
When you play the 'Patient game'.

First you get your research done,
Blood tests, and not just the one
And perhaps a scan or two.
But that wouldn't be up to you.
Got to keep your fitness up
To take it further that's a must!

Time goes by from check to check.
Your life is slowly changing track.
As a patient I suggest
Delegating is the best
If certain fitness still exists
Only show it when it fits!

Accepting helping hands
From kindly friends
Might protect you from a fall
But mainly is a joy for all.
A simple Thank You will not do
Brownie Points you hand out too!
Who could say no to such a treat?
Both sides happy, yes indeed.

Decisions

My poems come, I might just mention,
Without much thought and no intention
Triggered by a fallen tree
Or an insect I would see!

Then, my thoughts, I let them wander
From safe distance to wonder.
... until life's reality
Brutally descends on me.
What to do and how to act
Is a challenge and a fact.

Some decisions we do make,
In early life or even late,
Are rather hard for us to swallow.
But with time they get more mellow
And tough decisions soon will be
A very distant memory!
Then life's renewal every day
Should confirm them, I would say.
And with another pot of tea
Shared with friends and family,
Imbibing tons of energy
To have a dance or climb a tree!

Good surprises

Being the old lady peasant
I find planning not so pleasant.
I gladly leave it to my son,
Surprises can be so much fun!
It's my son, who organises
I just wait for good surprises.

And good they are, without exemption,
As shows our visit to Southampton.
A Professor there we meet,
His research is what we need.
He explains, communicates
Leading to the route to take.

He has a microscopic look
At my innards, surgeons took.
He researches, gives advice
.... and then he is, well, rather nice.
He can't go wrong, it's clear to me
As he likes my poetry!

Marigolds

The Easter colour, if you follow,
Is like the Daffodil, bright yellow,
With Crocus, Primrose, Buttercup
A sign that spring is coming up.

Marigolds are on my mind;
No, not the flowering kind,
But rubber gloves, they used of old
To do the dishes, I am told.
They help to put my stocking on,
Elasticated and so strong!
I work on him with all my might
Every morning, every night!

On Easter morning they gave up!
No Marigolds, that IS bad luck!
I ring my friends, is there a spare-
Pair of Marigolds somewhere?

The egg hunt, they gave up for me
To search the cupboards on one knee.
Easter with no eggs at all,
Instead it's Marigolds galore !
That shows me more than anything
The joys my lovely friend can bring!

A scar with personality

Another Op is on the card.
Another surgeon is in charge.
As first we meet in preparation
I feel a whiff of consternation
When, after years, I am surprised
To suddenly be recognized!

Unbeknown to me,
The surgeon I had never seen,
Did recognize me by my scar!
It used to be the face so far,
That would make us who we are,
More detailed now, hence the scar!

It's the suture on my tummy,
Must be special, rather funny!
A stich with personality,
High art of embroidery!
....."that's my work in ninety-two
No doubt, I do know you!"

Three surgeons

To catch the interest of three guys
Is amazing, in my eyes,
For a female of my age
Or at any other stage.

There they were deliberating
With their scalpels concentrating.
Yes, three surgeons took a look
And did everything they could.
They all studied are real bright
So, I am sure they got it right!

It's still amazing in my eyes
To get the interest of three guys!
It's just the thought, that feels so good
I was asleep, I couldn't look!

Recovery

When waking up, somewhat belated,
I found myself revived, elated!
The operation done and dusted
Helped by doctors skilled and trusted.

In' Recovery', I wake
... and such good care they take!
We even had some fun and laughter,
Followed by a dip there after.
Pain and no mobility
... a long road to recovery!
I am tired, cannot move...
And then the nurses come to prove
That I can get out of bed
And dare a hesitating step!
...a step that leads to new delights
Believing in a future bright!

The distraction

With great joy I do detect
Movement in my colon track!
A distraction, that it is!
All that boredom, I could miss.

Lying in my single room
Two pictures with a flowering bloom
On blank wall with clock above,
That isn't always quite enough.

You start thinking longingly
Of the ward-life you had seen.
I never noticed pictures there,
No private shower, to be fair!
But people.... action all day long,
There was the real- life going on!

I wonder, in my single room,
With two pictures still in bloom,
Is it the price of luxury...
To leave behind humanity?
...in rolls the lady with the tray!
She never is too far away,
With lovely chat and cup of tea
Is there a better place to be?

Shakespeare

Every time we meet,
My clever neighbour is a treat!
He even came to visit me
Where most men are too scared to be.
The hospital environment
Seems special, a predicament.

He brought for me a clever book
Prompting an astonished look.
As a peasant, reading is
A thing I try to give a miss.
But Shakespeare is a guy
You can't avoid, so do not try!

Will is a poet- colleague, so somehow,
A bit more I ought to know.
And there is a parallel
On which I really like to dwell.
About his name and how to write it
He constantly was undecided!
Isn't that compelling
A writer with uncertain spelling!

Our spelling talents...... here they meet
Tempting me to start and read!

SURVIVAL TRAY

BILL
Bryson
SHAKESPEARE

Home from hospital

Twice a day they dust the shelf,
I have a shower to myself!
The nurses are as kind as ever,
It couldn't have gone any better!

Now, that I leave my single room,
I can feel a lifting gloom...
Driving home, exploding spring
...I could sing...I could sing!
They hit my brain and make me mellow
The Rape- field's bright and striking yellow!

No more wall in front of me,
With two pictures I would see!
Oh, I glow with joy no end,
Driven by a trusted friend
To be embraced by Jack, the dog
Presenting me his latest log!
And last, not least,
My lovely geese!
They welcome me and greet...
Through their shiny orange beak.

Cod in parsley sauce

When coming out of hospital
Or not wanting to do bu**er all....
Then, take cod, the frozen kind,
In parsley sauce, it is a find!
Go open up the fridge
The cod, it is delish!
Microwaved and done,
'Supper ready everyone'!

I love cod, the frozen kind,
In parsley sauce, it is a find.
Hairy spells, there are aplenty,
When the fridge is cleared out, empty.
Think of the guests you asked before,
Forgot?... They are waiting at the door.
That's when the cod comes to the fore,
Frozen, cool, prepared to score!
Bless parsley sauce and cod in it
To his praise there is no limit!

COD IN PARSLEY
SAUCE

35

www.michelemeyer.net

Printed in Great Britain
by Amazon